STICK-TO-IT-IVENESS

STICK-TO-IT-IVENESS

Inspirations to Get You Where You Want to Go

Addie Johnson

Conari Press

First published in 2010 by
Red Wheel/Weiser, LLC
With offices at:
500 Third Street, Suite 230
San Francisco, CA 94107
www.redwheelweiser.com

ISBN: 978-1-57324-474-9
Library of Congress Cataloging-in-Publication Data
is available upon request.

Cover and text design by Jessica Dacher
Proofread by Erin Brenner
Typeset in Trade Gothic, Triplex, and French Iconic

Printed in Hong Kong
GW
10 9 8 7 6 5 4 3 2 1

NEVER NEVER NEVER

GIVE UP

— Winston Churchill

The three great essentials to achieve anything worthwhile are, first, hard work; second, stick-to-it-iveness; third, common sense.

— **Thomas A. Edison**

Hidden in Plain View

The key to accomplishing your life's work and living your wildest dreams is a secret hidden in plain view. It's a promise we make to ourselves and a road map to fulfill that promise, all wrapped into one package. Wherever someone achieves something worthwhile, whenever someone breathes life into a long-held dream, this singular, special key has opened the door. **Stick-to-it-iveness** is a funny word, some might say it's not even a real word, but it speaks for itself. Sticking to our inspirations, our values, our hopes and dreams. Sticking to our family and friends. Sticking to it even when others tell us to forget it. Sticking with it when we're facing tough times and when we aren't sure whether or not we can make it.

When we match stick-to-it-iveness with its natural companions, hard work and common sense, there's nothing we can't accomplish. We can all use a little inspiration to help us plant one foot in front of the other, to do what we came into this life to do. Here's the key, for you and to pass on to those you care about: perseverance, resolve, determination, doggedness, tenacity, staying power, steadfastness, dedication, persistence, commitment, fortitude, grit, endurance, resilience, guts, stamina. Here's to the power of stick-to-it-iveness!

"There is no use trying,"
said Alice: "one can't believe
impossible things."

"I dare say you haven't had much practice," said the Queen. "When I was your age, I always did it for half-an-hour a day. Why, sometimes I've believed as many as six impossible things before breakfast."

— **Lewis Carroll**

YOU'VE GOT TO BUMBLE FORWARD INTO THE UNKNOWN.

— Frank Gehry

Think you can't get there from here?
Make your own map.

Shackleton and the *Endurance*

One of the greatest stories of survival and perseverance ever told is that of Earnest Shackleton's polar expedition on the ship the *Endurance*. He set out with a crew of twenty-seven sailors and scientists attempting to be the first to cross the Antarctic by foot. As they neared the continent, the temperature plummeted and the *Endurance* became trapped in the Weddell Sea. After months spent on the frozen ship, the men realized that the hull would be crushed by pressure from the ice, and the men abandoned ship to camp on the drifting ice floes for several more months. Eventually they spotted open water and were able to sail their three lifeboats to Elephant Island, a desolate place with no settlement.

Knowing his men could never survive where they were, Shackleton decided to attempt an incredible seventeen-day, 800-mile journey, in freezing hurricane conditions, to the nearest civilization—South Georgia Island. They made the trip on the open sea in a lifeboat. When they got there, they still had to trek over mountains to reach the island's remote whaling station. There, Shackleton was able to organize a rescue team and return to Elephant Island to save all of the men they left behind.

Though the vessel *Endurance* was broken up on the ice, the members of her exhibition lived up to the name and endured almost beyond belief.

Do everything with a mind that lets go.
Do not expect praise or reward.
— Achaan Chah

Stick to it with courage, persevere with grace, keep your bearing, and hang in there. Do what needs to be done, and all will be well.

Farmers and fishermen, parents and teachers—all have the conviction to begin a series of arduous actions whose results lie in the far off and the unknown.

Faith is taking the first step even when you don't see the whole staircase.

— **Martin Luther King, Jr.**

Without discipline, there's no life at all.
— Katharine Hepburn

The great photographer Irving Penn was famous for spending hours, or even days, poring over hundreds of examples of whatever subject he'd chosen—lemons, mice, cigarette butts— before shooting the perfect one. All those long hours of work distilled into one perfect click of the shutter.

To love someone deeply gives you strength.
Being loved by someone deeply gives you courage.
— Lao Tzu

Love yourself, your family, and your community deeply and there's nothing you can't do.

Courage is fear holding
on a minute longer.
— George S. Patton

Hope for courage, but never expect to be freed
from fear. Gather up your fear and master it with
courage, and nothing can stop you.

Our virtues and our failings are
inseparable, like force and matter.
When they separate, man is no more.

— **Nikola Tesla**

To deny our failings is to tear apart the very heart and soul of who we are, and to give away our greatest potential power.

The heart that breaks open can
contain the whole universe.
— Joanna Macy

When a door closes, a window opens, and who knows where that will lead?

A knowledge of the path cannot
be substituted for putting one
foot in front of the other.

— **M. C. Richards**

Any map can show you the path up the mountain—
a straight or winding line on a piece of paper. But no
map knows the effort it takes to get there, the pitfalls
and challenges concealed in the rock, the heights of
experience waiting for you at the top.

I AM PREPARED TO GO ANYWHERE, PROVIDED IT BE FORWARD.

— David Livingstone

In hard times, sometimes a little forward motion is the only way to stay standing.

It is good to have an end to journey toward;
but it is the journey that matters, in the end.

— Ursula K. LeGuin

One step begins the journey.
The first may be lively and light;
the next may be plodding or timid.

DO NOT HESITATE.

In the rhythm of your paces, you
will discover that the journey is
the destination.

The three *h*'s for staying the course:

HABIT,

Create powerful habits through simple repetition.

HUMOR,

Lighten your load with laughter.

AND HOPE

Keep hope alive and you're unstoppable.

There must be more to life
than having everything!
— **Maurice Sendak**

Why does a kid with a room full of toys and games get bored? Remember that stick-to-it-iveness can be sticky fun. Get stuck on doing something you can love to do every day, and having less or more will matter but a little.

The three *e*'s for helping
someone else stick to it:

EMPATHIZE

EVALUATE

ENERGIZE

Look through their eyes, feel what they're feeling, and empathize.

Take the time to tell the truth, evaluating where they are and what they can change.

Sometimes all we need to keep going is a little boost of energy—an incentive, a kick in the pants, or a reminder of how much what we're doing really matters.

We gain strength, and courage, and
confidence by each experience in which we really
stop to look fear in the face . . . we must do
that which we think we cannot.
— **Eleanor Roosevelt**

Most of us have far more courage
than we ever dreamed we possessed.
— **Dale Carnegie**

Life shrinks or expands in
proportion to one's courage.
— **Anais Nin**

I am not afraid . . .
I was born to do this.
— **Joan of Arc**

This ain't fun. But you watch me, I'll get it done.
— Jackie Robinson

Jackie Robinson played his first minor league game on March 17, 1945. He was the first African American to play in the major leagues, debuting on April 15, 1947. People in the crowds and players on other teams sometimes jeered at Robinson, and he and his family received threats. But he kept going, helping the Dodgers finally win the World Series in 1955, and eventually retiring from the sport in 1957. His lifetime stick-to-it-iveness changed the face of professional sports forever.

No cakewalk.
No picnic.
No walk in the park.
Just get it done.

Get up tomorrow early in the morning,
and earlier than you did today,
and do the best that you can.

— Joan of Arc

An hour less sleeping, an hour less driving, an hour less watching TV; an hour more with family, an hour more walking, an hour more to finish that project close to your heart.

We realize that what we are accomplishing is a drop in the ocean. But if this drop were not in the ocean, it would be missed.

— **Mother Teresa**

A man, as a general rule, owes very little to what he is born with—a man is what he makes of himself.

— **Alexander Graham Bell**

Die when I may, I want it said of me by those who knew me best that I always plucked a thistle and planted a flower where I thought a flower would grow.

— **Abraham Lincoln**

This only is charity, to do all, all that we can.

— John Donne

A Story of
Hard Work, Stick-to-it-iveness, Common Sense . . . and Doggedness.

In the late summer of 2005 my mother's battle with colon cancer came to a head. As she was dying, my mother managed to pull together the most extraordinary group of friends and family, and I experienced more love and support condensed in that span of time than I had ever before.

Certainly my mother's battle over the years leading up to this time involved a juggling of tenacity and will power and a sense of figuring out purpose and staying power, but hers is actually the backdrop to my anecdote for you. As we all went about our days caring for her and trying to stay ahead of the constantly changing set of realities, practical and otherwise, certain aspects of daily life in the house went a little awry. Or, at least, unchecked.

Somehow, a 50 lb. bag of dog food had ended up in her bedroom.

I remember half-noticing it one day. At some point later in the day, on the umpteenth trip, I became aware that on every previous voyage across the room, the bag of dog food had seemed to have moved slightly. Not enough to notice each time, but now, late in the day, it was clear that the bag was well across the room from where it had started. I pondered this for all of a few seconds and continued on my way. The futility of my painstakingly meticulous schedule was beginning to sink in, as it was evident that Mum's circumstances were changing so rapidly they were "un-scheduleable." I could not control what was happening. What did it matter how this bag of dog food had ended up where it was or, indeed, that no one had thought to move it?

About 10 that night, I was in the bedroom again. In the dark there was a scrabbling and crunching. There was the bag of dog food, in the corner, farthest from the door to the bedroom. I went over to inspect and a sheepish but gleeful set of eyes greeted me. It was Wilton, our 8-lb. Chihuahua. Rescued by my husband earlier that year from the jaws of I-5, this was a dog who had spent his life, before we met him, surviving on the streets of Los Angeles, and who had on this day exhibited fine examples of Edison's Three Great Essentials To Achieving Anything Worthwhile in hauling five times his body weight across about 18 feet of a carpeted floor, undetected, to ensure that he got his dinner.

— **Francesca Faridany**

The Great Race

The Iditarod has been called "the last great race on earth." From Anchorage, in south central Alaska, to Nome on the western Bering Sea coast, each team of 12 to 16 dogs and their human musher cover over 1,150 miles in 10 to 17 days, crossing some of the roughest and most beautiful terrain in the world in sub-zero temperatures. No one can make the trip without dedicated training, thoughtful preparation, fierce willpower, and heroic stamina.

"It's not the size of the dog in the fight, it's the size of the fight in the dog."

— Mark Twain

Nothing earthly will make me give up my work in despair.

— David Livingstone

FEAR NOT!
WORK, WORK,
AND
WORK SOME MORE.

To thine own self be true, and it must follow, as the night the day, thou canst not then be false to any man.

— **William Shakespeare**

It is always sunrise somewhere; the dew is never dried all at once; a shower is forever falling; vapor is ever rising. Eternal sunrise, eternal dawn and gloaming, on sea and continents and islands, each in its turn, as the round earth rolls.

— John Muir

There will be a
new day, and enough
time to see and feel
and do all the things
we want to do.

Failure after long perseverance is much grander than never to have a striving good enough to be called a failure.

— **George Eliot**

Never a failure, always a lesson.
Trying is its own form of success.

> One man with courage is a majority.
> — Thomas Jefferson

Do the Right Thing

I love the story about A. J. Muste, who, during the Vietnam War, stood in front of the White House night after night with a candle—sometimes alone. A reporter interviewed him one evening as he stood there in the rain. "Mr. Muste," the reporter said, "do you really think you are going to change the policies of this country by standing out here alone at night with a candle?" A. J. responded, "Oh, I don't do this to change the country. I do this so the country doesn't change me."

— Andrea Ayvazian

When your bow is broken and your last arrow spent,
then shoot, shoot with your whole heart.
— **Zen saying**

Aim with your heart and you can't go wrong.

All of us need to be touched in the deepest
parts of our lives, to have our spirit uncapped.
If you uncap it, it will go everywhere.
That's why we're here.

— The Reverend Cecil Williams

True Perseverance

Helen Keller was born a normal child in 1880 in Alabama, and lost her sight and hearing as a result of severe illness when she was 18 months old. It was not until she was six that Anne Sullivan came to be her teacher, and within three years Keller could read and write in sign language and in Braille. Her spirit was uncapped. Sullivan remained a companion, translator, and friend for the rest of her pupil's life, attending Radcliffe College with Keller, who graduated cum laude in 1904. Keller became an author and lecturer, traveling the world and fighting for improvements in the education and life of the physically disabled.

Happiness is not a goal; it is a by-product.

— **Eleanor Roosevelt**

Work at your dream a little every day, and the by-product multiplies.

The principle thing in the world
is to keep the soul aloft.
— Gustave Flaubert

CHIN UP!
SPIRITS UP!
PULL YOUR SOCKS UP
AND THINGS START
TO LOOK UP!

When a person is willing and
eager, the gods join in.

— Aeschylus

Don't worry about time, energy, resources. Throw yourself into what you're doing and know that somebody's got your back.

EVERYTHING THAT IS NOT GIVEN IS LOST.

— Indian proverb

What are you saving it for?
Give it all you've got!

Penguin Parenting

Emperor penguins are the only animals strong enough to brave the winter ice and water in Antarctica, where they eat, breed, and raise their young. They clump together in huge, huddled masses to withstand the cold, each taking turns moving from the center of the group to the outside edge so everyone has a chance to get warm. After a several-week courtship, the female Emperor penguin lays one egg and then leaves, walking and scooting up to 50 miles across the ice to get to the open sea to eat and fish. Meanwhile, the male penguins keep the eggs balanced on their feet and under a warm layer of skin and feathers. They stand like that for 65 days, eating nothing the entire time. After two months, the mothers return to regurgitate food for the now-hatched chicks, and the fathers take off eagerly to go fishing at sea, making the same long journey over the ice and back to regurgitate more food for the chicks. Eventually, both parents can leave to go fishing and come back again until the chicks are big enough to make the journey themselves, and the cycle begins again.

Whenever you are confronted with an
opponent, conquer him with love.

— Gandhi

Love is the most powerful weapon. Besides, it's more fun that way.

I am only one; but still I am one. I cannot do everything, but still I can do something. I will not refuse to do the something I can do.

— Helen Keller

Paper Cranes

Sadako Sasaki was a two-year-old girl living in Hiroshima when the Allied Forces dropped an atomic bomb one mile from her family's home. The family survived and Sadako lived a normal life until she was twelve, when she was diagnosed with leukemia related to her radiation exposure. Inspired by a Japanese saying that folding 1,000 paper cranes meant your wish would be granted, she began to make the paper birds out of whatever paper she could find as well as paper brought by friends and other visitors to the hospital. Her mother later wrote, "She folded paper cranes carefully, one by one, using a piece of paper of advertisement, medicine, and wrapping. Her eyes were shining while she was folding the cranes, showing she wanted to survive by all means." Sadako died on October 25, 1955, and while her cranes did not save her life, the story of her dedication and endurance has made her an inspiring symbol of peace and hope for the world.

We can acknowledge that oppression will always be with us, and still strive for justice. We can admit the intractability of deprivation, and still strive for dignity. Clear-eyed, we can understand that there will be war, and still strive for peace. We can do that—for that is the story of human progress; that's the hope of all the world; and at this moment of challenge, that must be our work here on Earth.

— Barack Obama

When you get into a tight place and
everything goes against you, till it seems
as though you could not hang on a minute
longer, never give up then, for it is just the
place and time that the tide will turn.

— **Harriet Beecher Stowe**

If you think positively, you can always move forward ...

There is nothing either good or bad, but thinking makes it so.
— **William Shakespeare**

Much of the pain we encounter is due to our failure to understand reality. Too often our judgment and behavior are confined only to the level of appearances, and so we experience various kinds of suffering.
— **The Dalai Lama**

It is not the mountain we conquer but ourselves.
— **Edmund Hillary**

Sticking to It Through Millennia

The *welwitschia mirabilis* plant of South West Africa can live for up to 2,000 years in the middle of the desert and often goes ten years without a single drop of rain. There is nothing else like it, a plant that only ever produces one stem and two leaves, which grow continuously outward instead of upward. It thrives in temperatures over 100 degrees and survives even after people and animals tear away large portions of it for food. Here's to all of us enjoying that kind of perseverance and success.

Difficulties are just things
to overcome, after all.
— **Ernest Shackleton**

What fun would life be
without a few hurdles?

Keep Your Wits About You

There's a reason that Edison's three things are hard work, stick-to-it-iveness, and common sense. Without common sense, hard work and sticking to it can be a fool's errand, as in this story about a man named Billy from Paul Johnson:

One summer, the Department of Natural Resources poisoned the water of Bass Lake, WI, to kill all of the fish. It had become overpopulated with small, undesirable species, and the plan was to restock the lake the next summer. One day Herb drove by the lake and noticed Billy's truck parked by the dock. Billy was fishing. Herb said, "Billy, didn't you know they poisoned the lake? There are no fish." Billy replied, "Yeah, I know that, but I never catch anything anyway." He fished all day. While his stick-to-it-iveness was impressive, his common sense was lacking.

If You Believe...

Then again, what at first appears a fool's errand may be a wise person's journey. Don't forget that what makes sense to the general population may not make sense to you, and vice versa. So many times throughout history, people have said something was crazy, said it couldn't be done. They said it to Galileo when he told them the earth was round. They said it to Martin Luther King, Jr. about his dream of equality. They said it to Amelia Earhart about flying solo across the Atlantic. They said it to Mahatma Gandhi about overthrowing British colonial rule. When someone tells you something you believe in can't be done, that probably means *you're the one who's meant to do it.*

Fortitude is the marshal of thought, the armor of the will, and the fort of reason.
— **Francis Bacon**

Passion is the call to action, the fuel for dreams, the catalyst for triumph.

If you lose hope, somehow you lose the
vitality that keeps life moving, you lose that
courage to be, that quality that helps you
go on in spite of it all.

— **Martin Luther King, Jr.**

Success is not final, failure is not fatal:
it is the courage to continue that counts.

— **Winston Churchill**

Lord, make me an instrument of your peace;

where there is hatred, let me sow love;

where there is injury, pardon;

where there is doubt, faith;

where there is despair, hope;

where there is darkness, light;

and where there is sadness, joy.

— St. Francis of Assisi

WE MUST BUILD DIKES OF COURAGE TO HOLD BACK THE FLOOD OF FEAR.

— Martin Luther King, Jr.

Sea Change, Drop by Drop

From the start of the Montgomery Bus Boycott in 1955 until he was assassinated in 1968, Martin Luther King, Jr. worked tirelessly for the cause of freedom and justice and to bring an end to segregation. He endured threats to his family, his home was bombed, he was sent to jail many times. What now seems like an inevitable march to overthrowing the unfair and oppressive laws in the South was a hard-fought, day-by-day struggle that included many setbacks and almost unbearable opposition from all sides. This surely must have felt like a flood of fear, but in the end Dr. King and all those who worked for the cause were able to effect a sea change.

The monarch butterfly can travel up to 3,000 miles in its annual migration. Not bad for an insect with a four-inch wingspan who weighs less than a gram and only lives up to eight months.

California's redwood trees are among the world's tallest and oldest living trees, growing up to 368 feet and 1,500 years old (though the oldest discovered was thought to be over 3,000 years old). All that starting from a seed smaller than a pea.

By prevailing over all obstacles and
distractions, one may unfailingly arrive
at his chosen goal or destination.
— **Christopher Columbus**

Or maybe, arrive at a destination just as good—like say you're looking for a trade route to Asia and you stumble upon the Americas instead.

If we were logical, the future would be bleak, indeed. But we are more than logical. We are human beings, and we have faith, and we have hope, and we can work.

— Jacques Yves Cousteau

To hope is human;
to strive is in our nature;
to stick to it is a given.

I was happy in the midst of dangers and inconveniences.

— **Daniel Boone**

If you love
the journey,
happiness will
follow wherever
you lead.

IT MAY BE THAT THOSE WHO DO MOST, DREAM MOST.

— **Stephen Butler Leacock**

From Farm Hand to Franchise Founder

Colonel Harland Sanders had many jobs before founding the now-iconic Kentucky Fried Chicken franchise. From farm hand to practicing lawyer to owner of a series of motels and restaurants where he served his secret fried chicken recipe, he found himself at the age of 65 with a social security check and dwindling business at the restaurant he owned. He traveled the country in his trademark white suit with the dream of marketing his chicken to other restaurants—and was rejected over 1,000 times as he pitched his product. Through perseverance and willpower, he finally found a partner to work with. They launched the first Kentucky Fried Chicken site in 1952.

By perseverance the snail reached the ark.

— **Charles Spurgeon**

If you think you are too small to be effective,
you have never been in bed with a mosquito.

— **Betty Reese**

When things are going slowly, think of the ocean, whose steady rhythm wears cliffs into sandy beaches, wave by wave.

Perseverance, secret of all triumphs.

— Victor Hugo

It's not that you make mistakes, it's what you make of your mistakes.

That old saying "walk it off" has
deep meaning. If you get knocked down
by a 200-pound linebacker in a high
school game and your leg hurts, a good
coach will always say, "Walk it off!"
Same goes for heartbreak, or getting
flustered by a sudden change in plans,
or even just stubbing your toe.
Walk it off and work it out.

Never compare yourself to others, work to your personal best. And beyond.

Life is not easy for any of us. But what
of that? We must have perseverance and
above all confidence in ourselves. We must
believe that we are gifted for something
and that this thing must be attained.

— **Marie Curie**

If I'd observed all the rules,
I'd never have got anywhere.

— **Marilyn Monroe**

It takes courage to grow up and become who you really are.

— E. E. Cummings

For Those Who Wait

At age 94, the abstract painter Carmen Herrera, as reported in *The New York Times*, has become the "hot new thing in painting." She has painted in private since her late twenties and sold her first artwork at 89. Her good friend, the painter Tony Bechara, told her: "We have a saying in Puerto Rico. The bus—*la guagua*—always comes for those who wait." She responded, "Well, Tony, I've been at the bus stop for 94 years!"

New York City restaurant owner Jimmy Carbone has a favorite personal slogan: *Keep on keepin' on!* He reveals that you must say this at least ten times in a row with some rhythmic accompaniment: *Keep on keepin' on, keep on keepin' on, keep on keepin' on...*

TAP YOUR TOE.
CLAP YOUR HANDS.
BANG A PAN.
MARCH IN TIME.
KEEP ON KEEPING ON.

A heart to resolve, a
head to contrive,
and a hand to execute.
— Edward Gibbon

DREAM IT.
THINK IT.
DO IT.

A Story of Yearly Persistence

For many playwrights, to be accepted as a member of New Dramatists, an organization in New York City, is serious cachet. The word *new* in its name is somewhat misleading: there are many *old* (read: *emerging* to *established*) members, but most of them share the same story: many times applied, many times rejected, before finally, finally being admitted. Members are chosen by a committee that changes every year. It's just the luck of the draw: do the members of that year's particular panel respond to your work or not? Legend has it that one playwright applied so many times that by the time she got in, she'd already won a Pulitzer. This is what I was told when I applied and was rejected, year after year, sometimes skipping a year to make it year after every other year. I was annoyed, I was "over it," who needed them? But still I applied. Then, one year, someone asked me, "Are you applying this year?" The truth was, I honestly forgot to. The deadline was the next day. I thought, "Whatever." I walked my materials over to them. Six months (and countless—I don't care to count—years) later, on a Friday night, I got a call from Todd London, New Dramatists artistic director, telling me that the panel was offering me membership and asking me, rhetorically, if I'd accept. It was as if I'd applied for the first time. All those years I was rejected disappeared.

— **Daniel Reitz**

Perseverance is not a long race; it is many short races one after the other.

— **Walter Elliot**

Break it down, take it slow. Go step by step. Do what you can today; it's a new race tomorrow.

What one does is what counts and not
what one had the intention of doing.

— **Pablo Picasso**

The most effective way to do it, is to do it.

— **Amelia Earhart**

DO IT.
DO IT.
DO IT!
(AND DO IT AGAIN.)

Knowing trees,
I understand the
meaning of patience.
Knowing grass,
I can appreciate
persistence.

— **Hal Borland**

Surviving All Kinds of Weather

Nature will find a way in the harshest conditions. Think of the desert, where soil temperatures may rise to 150 degrees during the day but can drop to the freezing point or below at night. The air and the soil are often bone dry, and when rain falls it comes in torrents, creating flash floods that run off before even soaking into the soil. Mother Nature responds with innumerable varieties of the cactus plant, with its broad root systems (a five-inch-tall barrel cactus can have roots that reach out four to five feet) and leaves that retain water and repel with their sharp spikes anyone who might munch on them. Adaptations make it possible for the plants to thrive and persevere—an inspiration for anyone trying to hold on and flourish in a difficult climate.

Anything worth doing is worth doing poorly until you learn to do it well.

— **Steve Brown**

I never did anything worth doing by accident, nor did any of my inventions come by accident; they came by work.

— **Plato**

Anything worth doing is
worth doing slowly.

— Mae West

Anything worth doing is
worth overdoing.

— Mick Jagger

I know quite certainly that I myself have no special talent; curiosity, obsession, and dogged endurance, combined with self-criticism, have brought me to my ideas.

— **Albert Einstein**

The late Edward M. Kennedy is said to have told his 10-year-old grandson "Little Teddy," as he once told the boy's father, "Medium Teddy," ahead of him, that he could master the difficulties of learning the family tradition of sailing. "We might not be the best," he said, but "we can work harder than anyone."

When you're trying to achieve
an impossible goal, work as
if you're in charge and pray as
if God is in charge.

FOR US, THERE IS ONLY THE TRYING. THE REST IS NOT OUR BUSINESS.

— T. S. Eliot

For Louise Rosén, who sticks to it in high style and with enduring grace.

Special thanks to:
Francesca Faridany, Jimmy Carbone, Paul Johnson,
Gabra Zackman, Daniel Reitz, Amy Potozkin, Bonni Hamilton,
Caroline Pincus, Michele Kimble, Susie Pral, Jean Pral,
Mattie Tirey, Jan Johnson, Denise Reber

. . . and most of all to Daniel and Bailey Talbott